HAL•LEONARD
STRUMENTAL
PLAY-ALONG

AUDIO ACCESS
INCLUDED

Songs from Frozen, Tangled and Enchanted

CONTENTS

FROZEN

2 Do You Want to Build a Snowman?

4 For the First Time in Forever

13 In Summer

14 Let It Go

16 Love Is an Open Door

TANGLED

8 I See the Light

10 I've Got a Dream

17 Mother Knows Best

24 When Will My Life Begin

ENCHANTED

6 Happy Working Song

18 So Close

20 That's How You Know

22 True Love's Kiss

To access audio visit:
www.halleonard.com/mylibrary

Enter Code
7675-6858-6863-0162

Audio Arrangements by Peter Deneff

ISBN 978-1-4803-8722-5

Disney characters and artwork © Disney Enterprises, Inc.

**WALT DISNEY MUSIC COMPANY
WONDERLAND MUSIC COMPANY, INC.**

DISTRIBUTED BY

HAL•LEONARD® CORPORATION
7777 W. BLUEMOUND RD. P.O. BOX 13819 MILWAUKEE, WI 53213

In Australia Contact:
Hal Leonard Australia Pty. Ltd.
4 Lentara Court
Cheltenham, Victoria, 3192 Australia
Email: ausadmin@halleonard.com.au

Visit Hal Leonard Online at
www.halleonard.com

DO YOU WANT TO BUILD A SNOWMAN?

from Disney's Animated Feature FROZEN

CLARINET

Music and Lyrics by KRISTEN ANDERSON-LOPEZ
and ROBERT LOPEZ

Moderately

Harp

FOR THE FIRST TIME IN FOREVER

from Disney's Animated Feature FROZEN

Clarinet

Music and Lyrics by KRISTEN ANDERSON-LOPEZ
and ROBERT LOPEZ

HAPPY WORKING SONG

from Walt Disneys Pictures' ENCHANTED

Music by ALAN MENKEN
Lyrics by STEPHEN SCHWARTZ

CLARINET

I SEE THE LIGHT

from Walt Disney Pictures' TANGLED

Clarinet

Music by ALAN MENKEN
Lyrics by GLENN SLATER

poco rit.   a tempo

rit.   mp

I'VE GOT A DREAM

from Walt Disney Pictures' TANGLED

CLARINET

Music by ALAN MENKEN
Lyrics by GLENN SLATER

IN SUMMER
from Disney's Animated Feature FROZEN

Clarinet

Music and Lyrics by KRISTEN ANDERSON-LOPEZ
and ROBERT LOPEZ

LET IT GO
from Disney's Animated Feature FROZEN

CLARINET

Moderately
Piano

Music and Lyrics by KRISTEN ANDERSON-LOPEZ
and ROBERT LOPEZ

LOVE IS AN OPEN DOOR
from Disney's Animated Feature FROZEN

Clarinet

Music and Lyrics by KRISTEN ANDERSON-LOPEZ
and ROBERT LOPEZ

MOTHER KNOWS BEST

from Walt Disney Pictures' TANGLED

Music by ALAN MENKEN
Lyrics by GLENN SLATER

Clarinet

SO CLOSE
from Walt Disney Pictures' ENCHANTED

Clarinet

Music by ALAN MENKEN
Lyrics by STEPHEN SCHWARTZ

Moderately, with feeling

THAT'S HOW YOU KNOW

from Walt Disney Pictures' ENCHANTED

Music by ALAN MENKEN
Lyrics by STEPHEN SCHWARTZ

CLARINET

Moderate Calypso

TRUE LOVE'S KISS

from Walt Disney Pictures' ENCHANTED

Clarinet

Music by ALAN MENKEN
Lyrics by STEPHEN SCHWARTZ

WHEN WILL MY LIFE BEGIN

from Walt Disney Pictures' TANGLED

CLARINET

Music by ALAN MENKEN
Lyrics by GLENN SLATER